EXPLORING COUNTRIES

United States

MEGAN KOPP

MEDIA ENHANCED BOOKS
AV²
BY WEIGL™
ADDED VALUE • AUDIO VISUAL

www.av2books.com

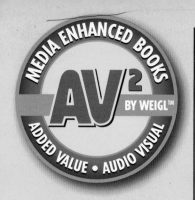

AV² provides enriched content that supplements and complements this book. Weigl's AV² books strive to create inspired learning and engage young minds in a total learning experience.

Your AV² Media Enhanced books come alive with...

Audio
Listen to sections of the book read aloud.

Key Words
Study vocabulary, and complete a matching word activity.

Go to **www.av2books.com**, and enter this book's unique code.

Video
Watch informative video clips.

Quizzes
Test your knowledge.

BOOK CODE

Q 2 6 8 6 8 9

Embedded Weblinks
Gain additional information for research.

Slide Show
View images and captions, and prepare a presentation.

AV² by Weigl brings you media enhanced books that support active learning.

Try This!
Complete activities and hands-on experiments.

... and much, much more!

Published by AV² by Weigl
350 5th Avenue, 59th Floor
New York, NY 10118
Website: www.av2books.com   www.weigl.com

Library of Congress Cataloging-in-Publication Data

Kopp, Megan.
 United States / Megan Kopp.
    p. cm. — (Exploring countries)
 Includes index.
 ISBN 978-1-62127-255-7 (hardcover : alk. paper) — ISBN 978-1-62127-261-8 (softcover : alk. paper)
 1. United States—Juvenile literature. I. Title.
 E156.K68 2013
 973—dc23   2012041036

Printed in the United States of America in North Mankato, Minnesota
1 2 3 4 5 6 7 8 9 17 16 15 14 13

052013
WEP040413

Project Coordinator Heather Kissock
Art Director Terry Paulhus

Photo Credits
Every reasonable effort has been made to trace ownership and to obtain permission to reprint copyright material. The publishers would be pleased to have any errors or omissions brought to their attention so that they may be corrected in subsequent printings.

Weigl acknowledges Getty Images as its primary image supplier for this title.

Contents

United States Overview

The greatest feature of the United States may be its variety. Located mostly on the continent of North America, this vast country includes plains, numerous mountain ranges, **lowlands**, **highlands**, deserts, Arctic **tundra**, and even volcanic islands. Its people are equally varied. **Indigenous** peoples have lived on the land for thousands of years. Today, as in the past, **immigrants** from all countries come to the United States with their own cultures. Plenty of natural resources and creative, productive workers have made the United States one of the world's wealthiest and most powerful nations.

Parades are held around the country on July 4th, when Americans celebrate Independence Day.

In the winter, skiers and snowboarders from all over the world come to the mountains of the western United States.

The White House in Washington, D.C., has been the home of every U.S. president except the country's first leader, George Washington.

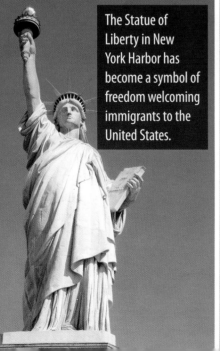
The Statue of Liberty in New York Harbor has become a symbol of freedom welcoming immigrants to the United States.

The indigenous people of Hawai'i share their culture through dancing.

Exploring the United States

The United States stretches from the Pacific Ocean in the west to the Atlantic Ocean in the east. It borders Canada to the north and Mexico to the south. With a total area of about 3.8 million square miles (9.8 million square kilometers), the United States is larger than every country except Russia and Canada. The country stretches as far as 2,700 miles (4,350 km) from east to west and about 1,600 miles (2,600 km) from north to south.

Mississippi River

N

UNI
STA

Grand Canyon

Mexico

Map Legend

United States

Land

Water

Mississippi River

Grand Canyon

Capital City

Everglades

250 Kilometers
SCALE
250 Miles

Grand Canyon

The Grand Canyon is a deep, narrow valley cut by the Colorado River in northern Arizona. The canyon spans nearly 280 miles (450 km). The deepest parts of the canyon are more than 1 mile (1.6 km) below the rim.

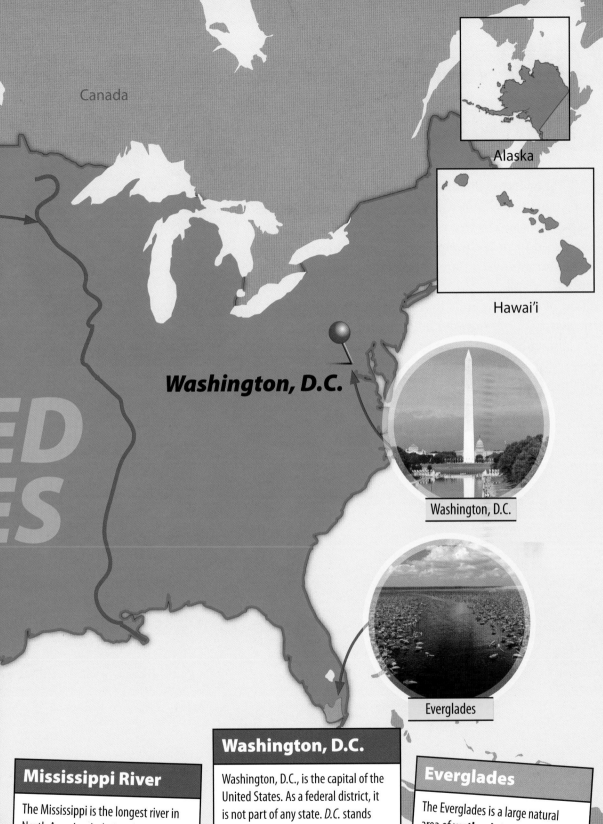

Canada

Alaska

Hawai'i

Washington, D.C.

Washington, D.C.

Everglades

Mississippi River

The Mississippi is the longest river in North America. It drains about one-eighth of the continent. Located in the central United States, it flows south from Minnesota to the Gulf of Mexico.

Washington, D.C.

Washington, D.C., is the capital of the United States. As a federal district, it is not part of any state. *D.C.* stands for "District of Columbia," after the explorer Christopher Columbus. Congress later added "Washington" to honor President George Washington.

Everglades

The Everglades is a large natural area of **wetlands** in southern Florida. Everglades National Park was created to protect part of this delicate **ecosystem**.

LAND AND CLIMATE

The United States has a huge central plain, tall mountains in the west, and hills and low mountains in the east. Separated from the mainland in the northwest is the mountainous state of Alaska, with its wide river valleys. The state of Hawai'i is a chain of rugged islands in the Pacific Ocean, more than 2,000 miles (3,200 km) southwest of California. The United States also has several island territories in the Caribbean Sea and the Pacific Ocean.

Delicate blue-violet wildflowers called harebells grow on the Alaskan tundra.

The hottest place on Earth is located in the United States. The temperature at Death Valley, California, once reached 134° Fahrenheit (57° Celsius).

Most of the large U.S. mountain ranges run north-south. They include the Rocky Mountains in western North America, the Sierra Nevada in eastern California, and the Appalachian Mountains in the eastern United States. The mountain ranges affect climate. The region east of the Rocky Mountains is much drier than areas west of the Rockies because air moving from west to east dries out as it rises and crosses the peaks. The climate is desertlike in the southwestern United States. The west coast has a mild climate year round. Hawai'i and southern Florida have warm tropical weather, while Alaska has an arctic climate. Most states have a continental climate, however, with cold winters and warm summers.

Wai'ale'ale Mountain in Hawai'i is the rainiest spot in the United States. Its annual average rainfall is 460 inches (117 centimeters). Arizona's Mojave Desert, however, receives just 2.6 inches (6.6 cm) of rain each year. Mount Washington in New Hampshire holds the record for the world's strongest surface wind, which once blew at 231 miles (372 km) per hour.

Land and Climate BY THE NUMBERS

20,320 Feet
Elevation of Mount McKinley, or Denali, the highest point in North America. (6,194 meters)

1,054 Square Miles
Land area of Rhode Island, the smallest U.S. state. (2,730 sq. km)

5 Number of Great Lakes totally or partly in the United States. They are Michigan, Superior, Huron, Erie, and Ontario.

6 Number of states in New England. They are Connecticut, Rhode Island, Massachusetts, Vermont, New Hampshire, and Maine.

PLANTS AND ANIMALS

1782
Year the bald eagle became the U.S. national emblem.

More Than 16,000
Number of native plant species in the United States.

 0 Number of native land reptiles and **amphibians** in Hawai'i.

Each **habitat** in the United States has many types of animals and plants. Grasses called blue grama grow on the Great Plains. Low shrubs and **lichens** cover the Arctic tundra regions. Cactus plants and various wildflowers grow in the desert habitats that stretch from southern California to Texas.

The country has both **coniferous** and **deciduous** forests. Trees commonly found in the United States include pine, fir, spruce, aspen, poplar, oak, and maple. California features both the world's tallest living tree and the world's oldest living tree. Hyperion is a coastal redwood that stands 379.1 feet (115.6 m) tall. Methuselah is a bristlecone pine tree that has lived for more than 4,700 years.

The United States is home to a variety of animals, from bats to badgers, foxes to ferrets, snakes to salamanders, and wolves to wolverines. More than 400 mammal and almost 300 reptile **species** live in the United States. There are also about 800 different types of fish and birds.

Several types of bears are found in the country. Polar bears hunt seals in Alaska, and grizzly bears run and swim in the western mountains. Black bears feed on animals and plants in both western and eastern forests.

The cougar is a large cat that lives in various habitats in the western United States. It is also known as the puma, mountain lion, or panther.

NATURAL RESOURCES

Things supplied by nature that have economic value are called natural resources. Rich in natural resources, the United States has vast areas of fertile soil for growing crops, plenty of water in certain regions, and forests full of timber. There are also huge deposits of coal, oil, natural gas, and other minerals.

About 740 million acres (300 million hectares) of land are covered by forests. The United States accounts for one-quarter of the world's production and use of forest products. Harvested trees include fir, pine, and oak.

Valuable iron ore deposits are mostly in Minnesota and Michigan. Missouri is known for its lead mines. Arizona, Utah, Montana, Nevada, and New Mexico supply copper to the world. Zinc is found in eastern states.

A leading coal producer, the United States mined more than 1 billion tons (907 million tonnes) in 2011. More than 90 percent of it was used to produce electricity. The country is also one of the world's biggest petroleum and natural gas producers. Texas is an oil and gas drilling center. Since 2008, North Dakota's oil industry has boomed, using a new drilling technology called **fracking**.

Natural Resources BY THE NUMBERS

More Than 1/4
Amount of the world's total coal reserves in the United States.

ABout 34%
Percent of the country's forestland owned by the U.S. government.

100,000
Number of Texas gas wells in 2011.

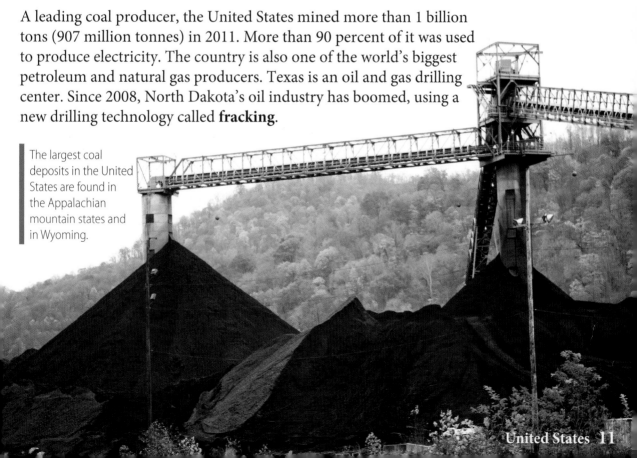

The largest coal deposits in the United States are found in the Appalachian mountain states and in Wyoming.

TOURISM

People visit natural, cultural, and historic attractions across all 50 U.S. states. Adventurers whale-watch off the coast of California. Families visit the world's most-popular theme park, the Magic Kingdom at Florida's Walt Disney World. Visitors to Massachusetts walk Boston's Freedom Trail to see sites related to the American Revolution, which took place from 1775 to 1783. Overall, the United States gets more foreign tourists than any other country in the world except France.

The country's most-visited tourist site is Times Square in New York City. Other popular destinations in New York include the Statue of Liberty, the Metropolitan Museum of Art, Central Park, and the 9/11 Memorial. This is a national tribute to those killed in the September 11, 2001, terrorist attacks on the United States.

Fisherman's Wharf has been the home of San Francisco's fishing fleets for almost 125 years. It is also a popular tourist destination, with seafood restaurants, museums, and shopping.

The 9/11 Memorial is on the site of the World Trade Center's twin towers, which were destroyed in 2001. The names of all the victims of the terrorist attacks are listed on bronze panels around two reflecting pools.

Landmarks in Washington, D.C., include the White House, Lincoln Memorial, Washington Monument, and Vietnam Veterans Memorial. Some tourist attractions in San Francisco, California, are the Golden Gate Bridge, Lombard Street's crooked path, and Fisherman's Wharf. Visitors to Los Angeles, the entertainment capital of the world, can tour movie studios. In the east, ski resorts and autumn leaves bring tourists to Vermont and New Hampshire.

National, state, and other parks are plentiful in the United States. Great Smoky Mountains National Park attracts the most visitors each year, at close to 9 million people. Other popular destinations include Grand Canyon, Yosemite, and Yellowstone national parks. Every year, more than 1 million people visit Pennsylvania's Gettysburg National Military Park. It is the site of one of the most important battles of the Civil War, the conflict over slavery between the northern and southern states that lasted from 1861 to 1865.

Huge crowds flock to Indiana each May for the Indianapolis 500 auto race. People from around the world enjoy the street celebrations and costumes of Mardi Gras in New Orleans, Louisiana. The big-name shows and casinos in Las Vegas, Nevada, draw millions of visitors each year.

Tourism BY THE NUMBERS

MORE THAN 40

Number of museums in the Boston area.

128 Miles Per Hour

Speed of the fastest roller coaster in the United States, at Six Flags Great Adventure in New Jersey. (206 km per hour)

17 Million

Number of people who visit the Magic Kingdom at Walt Disney World each year.

The Indianapolis 500 takes place on a 2.5-mile (4-km) oval called the Indianapolis Motor Speedway. The cars reach speeds of more than 150 miles (240 km) per hour.

INDUSTRY

The United States manufactures more products than any other country in the world except China. States in the Upper Midwest, such as Michigan, Ohio, and Indiana, are the center of the automobile industry. China is the only country that produces more motor vehicles than the United States. Manufacturing is also important in northeastern states. In recent years, many factories have opened in the South. Raw materials and finished goods are shipped across the country and around the world. There are close to 4 million miles (6.4 million km) of U.S. highways and almost 150,000 miles (240,000 km) of railway lines to transport products.

The midwestern United States has been called the nation's breadbasket because its farms feed so many people. Large crops of wheat, corn, and oats are grown here. Farms and ranches cover more than 90 percent of the land in North Dakota. The West is known for its cattle industry. Today's farmers and ranchers rely on high-tech machinery and equipment. Although nearly half of the country's land is used for farming, agriculture employs less than 1 percent of the country's workforce.

In Alaska, major industries include petroleum and fishing. The United States is one of the world's largest producers of fish products. In 2011, the country **exported** close to 1.5 million tons (1.3 million tonnes) of fish products. Exports totaled more than $5 billion.

Ford, General Motors, and Chrysler are the largest U.S. automakers. General Motors makes luxury Cadillac cars, first produced in 1902.

GOODS AND SERVICES

Goods made or grown in the United States include electronics products, iron and steel, airplanes, processed food, fresh vegetables, and fruits such as Washington apples and Florida oranges. However, most people in the United States provide services rather than manufacture goods. Service industries include banking and finance, communications, tourism, information technology, wholesale and retail trade, education, health care, and government. More than one of every four new jobs created between 2010 and 2020 will be related to health care and social assistance.

In the United States, about 7.5 million jobs are directly related to tourism and travel. In 2011, this field added $1.9 trillion to the U.S. economy. In many states, tourism is one of the fastest areas of growth. It is the largest income-producing activity in Florida.

Goods and Services BY THE NUMBERS

ABOUT 75%
Percentage of Minnesotans working in service industries.

3.2 MILLION

Number of teachers who work in U.S. public schools.

13 Billion POUNDS
Size of the potato crop each year in Idaho, which grows more potatoes than any other state. (5.9 billion kilograms)

In Hawai'i, more than 90 percent of workers are employed in service industries. These people include waiters and other restaurant workers.

INDIGENOUS PEOPLES

For thousands of years, American Indians were the only people living in what is now the United States. The first people were hunters who came to North America from Asia at least 15,000 years ago. Many scientists believe that the Inuit, or Eskimo, people of Alaska also came from Asia. The first people to live in Hawai'i were Polynesians, who traveled by canoe for thousands of miles from islands in the South Pacific.

In the past, most American Indians lived in small villages and relied on hunting or farming. The main crops were corn, beans, and squash. In the Southwest, the Ancestral Puebloan people built large cliff dwellings. Across the Great Plains, tribes followed the seasonal movements of the **bison** herds. In the Midwest, people of the Mississippian culture built large towns.

Several thousand different tribes were living in North America when the first Europeans arrived. At first, the Indians did not realize how great a threat European settlers were to their way of life. As the number of settlers grew, conflicts arose.

European explorers and settlers brought new diseases to North America. Many American Indians died from these diseases. Others died in wars with settlers and, later, in conflicts with U.S. soldiers. Over time, most American Indian groups were forced to give up their traditional lands and move to **reservations**.

American Indian groups try to preserve traditions at gatherings called powwows.

THE AGE OF EXPLORATION

Vikings from Greenland were the first Europeans to reach the North American mainland. Led by explorer Leif Eriksson, the Vikings reached eastern Canada and possibly northern New England around the year 1000. They did not establish permanent settlements and soon returned home.

Christopher Columbus, an Italian navigator sent by Spain, set out to find a short route to the Far East in 1492. He landed just off the North American mainland in today's Bahamas and claimed the land for Spain. Europeans soon understood that they had found a new land that offered opportunity for wealth and power.

In the 1500s, Spanish explorers moved into what is now the southeastern and western United States. Spain took control of Florida and large areas of land west of the Mississippi River. In 1565, Spanish settlers founded St. Augustine, Florida, the oldest permanent European settlement in today's United States. Spain also founded **missions** and other settlements in California and other parts of the West.

The Age of Exploration BY THE NUMBERS

3 Number of ships in Christopher Columbus's fleet in 1492.

21 Number of missions Spanish priest Junípero Serra and others set up in California between 1769 and 1833 to spread the Christian religion to American Indians.

1524 Year Italian navigator Giovanni da Verrazzano, sailing for France, became the first European to explore present-day New York Harbor and Narrangansett Bay.

Explorer Christopher Columbus first sighted American land on October 12, 1492. Many U.S. states have made the second Monday in October a legal holiday to commemorate the event.

EARLY SETTLERS

I n 1607, the first permanent English settlement in North America was founded in Jamestown, Virginia. A group of settlers, known as Pilgrims, established the second permanent English **colony** in Plymouth, Massachusetts, in 1620. They sailed on a ship called the *Mayflower* in search of religious freedom.

A seaworthy replica of the original *Mayflower* is docked in Plymouth, Massachusetts. Its overall length measures more than 100 feet (30 m).

In the following years, more settlers came and new colonies were established near the eastern coast. Most colonists were English, but the settlers also included people from the Netherlands, Sweden, France, Germany, Scotland, and Ireland. Many Africans were captured from their homeland and brought to the colonies as slaves. From 1609 to 1664, the Netherlands controlled the Hudson River valley. During that time, Dutch businessmen set up trading posts and towns as part of a colony called New Netherland. Unable to defend it, however, they surrendered control to England. By 1700, about 250,000 English settlers and other people of European descent were living in what is now the eastern United States.

The first European settlement in today's New York City was established in the 17th century by the Dutch West India Company. It was called New Amsterdam and served as the capital city of New Netherland.

The early settlers in today's United States faced great hardship and danger. Food was often scarce, and disease was common. Over time, however, the colonists began to prosper. Many established small family farms. In the South, **plantations** were run with slave labor. Towns were built, roads were cleared through forests, and small industries began to develop. The population continued to grow.

By the mid-1700s, most of the settlements had been formed into 13 British colonies. They were New Hampshire, Massachusetts, Connecticut, Rhode Island, New York, New Jersey, Pennsylvania, Delaware, Maryland, Virginia, North Carolina, South Carolina, and Georgia. Each colony had a royal governor appointed by the British government and a legislature.

In many parts of the South, African slaves of all ages worked the fields to pick and clean cotton for their owners.

POPULATION

In 1790, seven years after gaining independence, the United States held its first **census**. The results showed that there were just under 4 million people living in the country. By 1900, the population had reached 76 million. According to a 2013 Census Bureau estimate, the U.S. population is more than 315 million.

The U.S. population is not evenly spread out across the country. The largest numbers of people live in the East, along the West Coast, and in large cities. The nine states of California, Texas, New York, Florida, Illinois, Pennsylvania, Ohio, Michigan, and Georgia have about 50 percent of the total U.S. population. Wyoming has the smallest population of any state. Alaska has the lowest population per square mile (sq. km).

Nationwide, about 84 percent of people live in or near cities. The U.S. city that has the largest population is New York City, with about 8.2 million people. The population of Los Angeles is just under 4 million. Chicago's population is close to 3 million.

20 BILLION

Population count of New York–Newark, New Jersey, the world's fourth-largest urban area, after Tokyo, Japan; Delhi, India; and Mexico City, Mexico

More Than 37 Million

Number of residents in California, the most-populated U.S. state.

In New York City, so many people live in such a small area that traffic jams, especially with taxi cabs, are common.

POLITICS AND GOVERNMENT

During the American Revolution, the 13 colonies fought against the British for their independence. Colonial representatives announced their separation from Great Britain by signing the Declaration of Independence in 1776. The U.S. **Constitution**, completed in 1787, outlined how the new country's government would work. This document created the executive, legislative, and judicial branches of the federal, or national, government. Each branch has specific powers and duties to ensure a balance of power. The Constitution tries to prevent any one branch from becoming too powerful.

The executive branch is headed by a president, elected every four years. Voters made history in 2008 by electing U.S. senator Barack Obama. He became the first African-American president. The legislative branch includes two houses of Congress. They are the House of Representatives and the Senate. There are 435 elected members of the House, voted in every two years. The Senate has 100 members, two from each state, who are elected every six years. The judicial branch is made up of the U.S. Supreme Court, with a chief justice and eight other justices, as well as other federal courts.

The Senate and the House of Representatives meet in the U.S. Capitol in Washington, D.C.

CULTURAL GROUPS

The United States has always been a country of immigrants. It is often called a melting pot of different cultures and languages. English is the principal language. Spanish is the second-most-common spoken language, followed by Chinese.

Red paper lanterns are part of most Chinese New Year celebrations. The color red represents good fortune.

Though most Americans speak English, dress similarly, and eat the same types of food, many citizens also take pride in their cultural origins. The largest celebration of Polish culture in the United States is held each year in Milwaukee, Wisconsin. Mexican Americans around the country celebrate their heritage on Cinco de Mayo, Spanish for "fifth of May." Irish Americans observe the cultural and religious holiday Saint Patrick's Day on March 17. Parades are held in cities around the country. The first Nisei Week Japanese Festival in Los Angeles took place in 1934. Many people celebrate Diwali, the Hindu festival of lights.

For more than 50 years, workers in Chicago, Illinois, have dyed the Chicago River green to celebrate Saint Patrick's Day. About 400,000 spectators view the city's parade and watch the river turn green every year.

During the 1800s and early 1900s, most immigrants arriving in the United States came from Europe. From 1845 to 1860, more than 100,000 immigrants arrived in the country every year. The largest numbers were from Germany and Ireland. In the late 19th and early 20th centuries, millions of new residents came to the United States, many of them from areas in southern and eastern Europe. These immigrants made major contributions to the economic growth of the United States.

In recent decades, most immigrants have come from Latin American and Asian countries. **Hispanic** Americans now make up more than 16 percent of the U.S. population. They are one of the country's fastest-growing cultural groups. About 5 percent of the population is Asian American, including people of Chinese, Indian, Filipino, and Vietnamese descent. There are 39 million African Americans, who make up about 13 percent of the population.

People in the United States follow many different faiths. About half of all Americans are Protestant. Almost one-fourth of the population is Roman Catholic, and about 2 percent of Americans follow the Jewish faith. A growing number of Americans are Muslims, or people who follow Islam.

50 Million
Number of Hispanic Americans. Almost two-thirds are people of Mexican heritage.

12 Million
Number of people who passed through the Ellis Island immigration station in New York City from 1892 to 1924, planning to make the United States their home.

1/4 Fraction of Asian Americans who are of Chinese origin.

Some of New York's Hispanic population celebrate Cinco de Mayo with an annual street parade featuring traditional Mexican dance and music performances.

ARTS AND ENTERTAINMENT

American literature is read around the world, in all languages. It includes Henry David Thoreau's writings about nature, Walt Whitman's poetry, Ernest Hemingway's *The Old Man and the Sea*, and Mark Twain's *Adventures of Huckleberry Finn*. Millions of people have enjoyed *The Joy Luck Club*, written by Chinese-American Amy Tan, and novels about the African-American experience by Toni Morrison, winner of the Nobel Prize for literature in 1993.

Toni Morrison grew up in a large working-class family in Ohio. Her novels draw on the stories, songs, and folktales she learned in childhood.

The play *Lion King* opened in New York City in 1997. The inventive musical, full of colorful costumes and giant puppets, continues to be one of New York's longest-running shows.

American music is creative and varied. Musicals on the stage became very popular in the 1940s and 1950s, and they still draw large audiences in New York City's Broadway theater district. American country music started in the southern United States and the Appalachian Mountains during the 1800s. Country music stars such as Carrie Underwood and Blake Shelton sell millions of records each year. Pop superstar Taylor Swift began her career as a country music singer. Other uniquely American musical styles include soul music, a form of African-American rhythm and blues, and hip-hop, which came from the inner cities.

The company of U.S. inventor Thomas A. Edison developed a projector for showing motion pictures in the 1890s. By the time World War I had ended in 1918, movies coming from the Hollywood district of Los Angeles were being seen around the world. Today, comic book heroes come to life on the big screen in movies such as *The Avengers*, *The Dark Knight Rises*, and *The Amazing Spider-Man*.

Since the 1950s, television has been a part of American popular culture. Today, 99 percent of homes in the United States have at least one television. More than 65 percent of all homes in the country have three or more TV sets.

Singer-songwriter Taylor Swift has sold more than 26 million albums worldwide. In 2011, Swift had 11 separate tracks on the U.S. Hot 100. That is the most ever for a female artist.

SPORTS

Playing and watching sports has always been a part of American life. In the early part of the 20th century, fans cheered football's Red Grange, boxing's Jack Dempsey, golf's Bobby Jones, and baseball's Babe Ruth. Today, sports fans continue to have idols. They include basketball forward LeBron James, tennis player Serena Williams, football quarterback Tom Brady, soccer forward Alex Morgan, and baseball infielder Miguel Cabrera.

Baseball grew out of an 18th-century British game called rounders. The first baseball game with rules similar to today's was played in New Jersey in 1846. In 1903, Major League Baseball held its first championship, the World Series. Today, the major leagues have 30 teams and tens of millions of fans.

Basketball is the only major sport completely invented in the United States. In 1891, physical education instructor James Naismith hung two peach baskets at the ends of a gym in Springfield, Massachusetts, and gave players a soccer ball to throw into the baskets. By the 1900s, the game had spread around the world. Young players in driveways and public parks all over the United States practice hard in hopes of becoming a star in the National Basketball Association (NBA) or the Women's NBA.

Alex Morgan helped the U.S. women's soccer team win a gold medal in the 2012 Olympics.

LeBron James plays for Florida's Miami Heat. In 2013, at age 28, he became the youngest NBA player to score 20,000 points in his career.

Football is the most popular spectator sport in the United States. Every Sunday in the fall, millions of Americans watch their favorite National Football League (NFL) team on television. The Super Bowl, the NFL's championship game, is the most-watched event on television each year. Top entertainers perform during the Super Bowl halftime show.

Many Americans enjoy watching college sports. The most popular are football and basketball. Every spring, basketball fans watch the best men's and women's college teams compete in month-long tournaments, called March Madness, to determine the national champions. College football teams with the best records during the fall regular season play against one another in "bowl games" every December and January. The Bowl Championship Series (BCS) title game decides the national champion.

Each Super Bowl names a Most Valuable Player. Past winners include Joe Flacco of the Baltimore Ravens, who threw three touchdown passes to lead his team to victory in 2013.

Sports BY THE NUMBERS

MORE THAN 100 MILLION Number of people who watch the Super Bowl on TV.

ABOUT 16,000 Total number of golf courses in the United States.

1947 Year that Jackie Robinson became the first African American allowed to play on a Major League Baseball team.

Mapping the United States

We use many tools to interpret maps and to understand the locations of features such as cities, states, lakes, and rivers. The map below has many tools to help interpret information on the map of the United States.

Mapping Tools

- The compass rose shows north, south, east, and west. The points in between represent northeast, northwest, southeast, and southwest.

- The map scale shows that the distances on a map represent much longer distances in real life. If you measure the distance between objects on a map, you can use the map scale to calculate the actual distance in miles or kilometers between those two points.

- The lines of latitude and longitude are long lines that appear on maps. The lines of latitude run east to west and measure how far north or south of the equator a place is located. The lines of longitude run north to south and measure how far east or west of the Prime Meridian a place is located. A location on a map can be found by using the two numbers where latitude and longitude meet. This number is called a coordinate and is written using degrees and direction. For example, the city of Los Angeles would be found at 34°N and 118°W on a map.

Map of the United States

MAP LEGEND
- ★ Capital City
- ● City
- Body of Water
- --·--·-- Country Border
- ——— State Border

Map It

Using the map and the appropriate tools, complete the activities below.

Locating with latitude and longitude

1. Which state is found at 40°N and 77°W?
2. What lake is located at 37°N and 110°W?
3. Which large city is found on the map using the coordinates at 47°N and 122°W?

Distances between points

4. Using the map scale and a ruler, calculate the approximate distance between the cities of Chicago and Houston.
5. What is the approximate width of mainland United States from the Pacific Ocean in the west to the Atlantic Ocean in the east?
6. Using the map scale and a ruler, find the approximate length of the border between Arizona and New Mexico.

SCALE

Longitude & Latitude
USA
Other Countries

0   500 km

0   500 mi

Quiz Time

Test your knowledge of the United States by answering these questions.

1 Which oceans border the United States on the west coast and the east coast?

2 How big is the United States from north to south?

3 Which desert in Arizona receives just 2.6 inches (6.6 cm) of rain each year?

4 What type of bird is the national emblem?

5 What is the current population of the United States?

6 Name two Italian navigators who explored the Americas.

7 What was the name of the group of English settlers that sailed on the *Mayflower*?

8 What year did the United States declare independence from Great Britain?

9 Who won the Nobel Prize for literature in 1993?

10 Which popular sport was invented in the United States?

ANSWERS

1. Pacific and Atlantic
2. 1,600 miles (2,600 km)
3. Mojave Desert
4. Bald eagle
5. More than 315 million
6. Christopher Columbus and Giovanni da Verrazzano
7. Pilgrims
8. 1776
9. Toni Morrison
10. Basketball

Key Words

amphibians: animals that live both on land and in the water

bison: a large western North American animal with short curved horns and a shaggy mane

census: a count of all the people who live in a certain area

colony: land outside its borders that a country claims and governs

commonwealths: political units with local self-government but united with the United States

coniferous: evergreen trees and shrubs that have cones

constitution: a country's basic laws, which state the rights of the people and the powers of the government

deciduous: trees that lose their leaves every year in a certain season

ecosystem: communities of living things and resources

exported: sent to another country for trade or sale

fracking: a drilling technique that uses liquid under high pressure to release natural gas from rocks far below ground

habitat: the place where an animal or plant is usually found

highlands: elevated lands

Hispanic: referring to people who trace their origins to a Spanish-speaking culture

immigrants: people who move to a new country or area to live and work

indigenous: native to a particular area

lichens: plants that consist of a fungus and an algae growing together

lowlands: areas of low, flat land

missions: settlements established to teach religion to indigenous peoples

plantations: large farms that grow crops to be sold and that often are worked by people who live on the farm

reservations: areas of land set aside by the government for American Indians

species: groups of individuals with common characteristics

tundra: flat land in which soil below the surface is always frozen and only small plants can grow

wetlands: lowland areas that are often covered by or soaked with water

Index

Log on to www.av2books.com

AV² by Weigl brings you media enhanced books that support active learning. Go to www.av2books.com, and enter the special code found on page 2 of this book. You will gain access to enriched and enhanced content that supplements and complements this book. Content includes video, audio, weblinks, quizzes, a slide show, and activities.

AV² Online Navigation

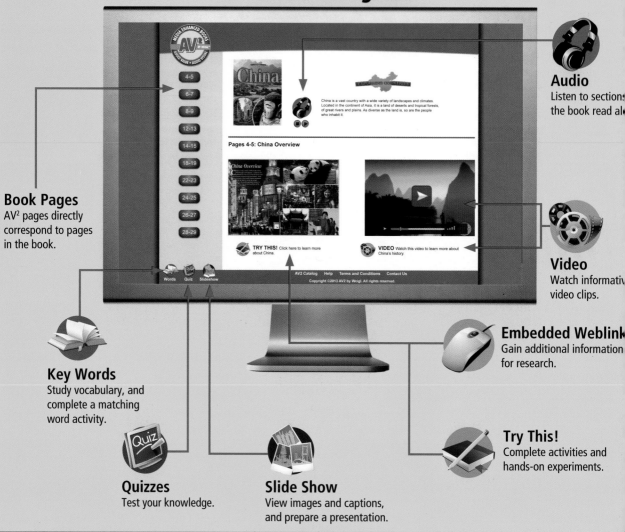

Audio
Listen to sections of the book read aloud.

Book Pages
AV² pages directly correspond to pages in the book.

Video
Watch informative video clips.

Key Words
Study vocabulary, and complete a matching word activity.

Embedded Weblinks
Gain additional information for research.

Try This!
Complete activities and hands-on experiments.

Quizzes
Test your knowledge.

Slide Show
View images and captions, and prepare a presentation.

AV² was built to bridge the gap between print and digital. We encourage you to tell us what you like and what you want to see in the future.

Sign up to be an AV² Ambassador at www.av2books.com/ambassador.